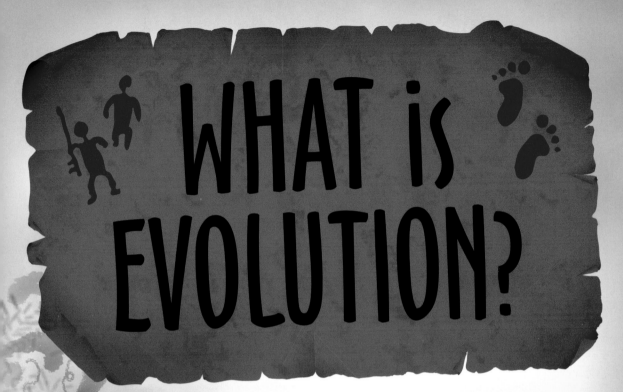

WHAT is EVOLUTION?

Louise Spilsbury
Mike Gordon

WAYLAND

First published in Great Britain in 2015
by Wayland

Copyright © Wayland, 2015

Editor: Julia Adams
Designer: Alyssa Peacock
Consultant: Tom Jackson

Dewey number: 576.8-dc23

ISBN 978 0 7502 9210 8
Library eBook ISBN 978 0 7502 9464 5
10 9 8 7 6 5 4 3 2 1

Wayland, an imprint of Hachette Children's Group
Part of Hodder & Stoughton
Carmelite House
50 Victoria Embankment
London EC4Y 0DZ

An Hachette UK Company
www.hachette.co.uk
www.hachettechildrens.co.uk

Printed and bound in China

CONTENTS

WHAT IS EVOLUTION?

Have you ever wondered why there are so many different types of living things on our planet and how they all got here? Or looked at a bird's sharp beak, a rabbit's long ears or a cat's curved claws and wondered how these animals got features that are so well-suited to their lives?

THE VARIETY OF LIFE

The world is full of an amazing variety of plants and animals, from the tiniest fungi to the largest whales. Did you know that there are 300,000 types, or species, of flowering plants alone? Or that scientists estimate there are about 9 million different species on Earth, many of which have not even been identified yet?

Each one of these millions of different species is incredibly well-suited to the habitat in which it lives. Cacti can survive in deserts where most other plants would shrivel and die within hours, and a gibbon's long arms seem

custom-made for swinging through forest trees. Seaweed thrives in salty seas that would dry out and kill other plants, and a polar bear's body fat and thick fur enable it to live in icy conditions that would freeze many other animals. Evolution is the scientific explanation for how this incredible biodiversity — or variety of life — came to be.

Biodiversity is the variety of plant and animal life in the world — and there is a lot of variety!

4

THE THEORY OF EVOLUTION

Scientists began developing the theory of evolution in the eighteenth century. Until this time, the world's cultures and religions had different ideas and beliefs about how living things were created, and many still adhere to those beliefs today. In scientific terms, evolution is the process by which different kinds of living things developed from earlier forms during the history of the Earth. It explains how living things can and have changed over time and how they developed into the many different species we see today on our planet. The basic idea behind evolution is that all the different species have evolved from life forms that first developed about 3.5 billion years ago (the Earth is approximately 4.5 billion years old). Evolution is supported by lots of evidence that has been collected by different experts and scientists for over 150 years.

FIRST LIFE FORMS

Most scientists agree that the first forms of life on Earth were tiny bacteria that were much, much simpler than any living things around today. These bacteria most likely developed in the murky seas and volcanic pools that formed early in the planet's history. Some types of bacteria released oxygen, and it was this that helped more complex organisms to start to evolve.

Until life began to develop on Earth around 3.5 billion years ago, our planet was a lonely, empty place. The story of evolution is the story of life on Earth.

EARLY IDEAS OF EVOLUTION

In the eighteenth century, scientists started studying the natural world in new depths. They grouped and classified species based on their similarities and differences. Through seeing patterns of relatedness, they started to question the long-held belief that God created all species, and whether in fact species change and new species develop over time...

CLASSIFYING THE LIVING WORLD

In around 1735, Swedish scientist Carl Linnaeus came up with the system for classifying and naming any living thing. We still use it to this day. He gave each plant and animal a specific name, so that everyone could identify it and scientists from different places could easily discuss it. Each living thing has a genus name, followed by a species name, both in Latin. A genus name is like a surname and species is a specific name. So, a grey wolf shares its genus name — *Canis* — with a few other members of the dog family, such as coyotes and jackals, but adding its species name — *Canis lupus* — describes only the grey wolf.

Early humans classified the plants and animals they found as safe or harmful. Since Linnaeus we have used a more sophisticated system!

DEFINING A SPECIES

A species is a group of animals or plants that share the same characteristics. The species that pet cats belong to almost all have sharp teeth, retractable claws, fur, a tail and the same number of toes. Organisms of the same species can also reproduce together. So, while a rose cannot breed with a cabbage, because they are different species, it can produce seeds with another rose, even if they look quite different.

NEW THEORIES

Linnaeus believed that he was simply describing the order of life created by God. But by using his system, along with plant and animal fossils found at this time, it became easier for scientists to see which living things were related and to tell if specimens they found were new to science or if they were remains of species that no longer existed. Scientists started to look for an explanation of how living things had changed over time.

The French naturalist G.L. Buffon had a theory that the Earth had a long history, and that life forms could have been generated from unorganised matter in the Earth's changing environments through time. The French naturalist Lamarck believed that a characteristic used a lot becomes bigger and stronger, while unused ones eventually disappear, and that improvements can be passed on to offspring. But if this were the case, why don't runners all have babies with muscular legs? Such scientists may have got it slightly wrong, but they opened the door for the famous Charles Darwin to come up with the theory of evolution.

When scientists studied fossils of animals that were new to science and compared them to Linnaeus's classification system, they realised these beasts no longer existed and that living things had, in fact, changed over time.

DID YOU KNOW?

Scientists have gone on using Linnaeus's system to name new species, and today there are about 1.9 million named species. However, large numbers of animals and plants have not been studied yet, and the actual number of species on the planet may be anywhere from 3 to 100 million!

DARWIN'S DARING DISCOVERY

Charles Darwin's interest in science and nature was partly inspired by his grandad, Erasmus Darwin. Erasmus studied nature and fossils and in 1794 had written about his ideas that all life developed from small, microscopic molluscs. So, in 1831 when the then 22-year-old Charles Darwin joined a five-year voyage aboard a ship called the HMS *Beagle*, sailing to South America to make maps of coastlines, it was to study nature and to explore some of these ideas.

WILD WORLD

During the trip Darwin saw some incredible wildlife, including large lizards that swam in the sea, birds with bright blue feet and sharks with hammer-shaped heads. He even rode on the back of a giant tortoise! While aboard, he studied the work of geologist Charles Lyell, who believed that the Earth was millions of years old, and that over time it had changed very slowly. If rocks were very old, then the fossils found in the rocks, and therefore life itself, must be very old, too. Darwin became convinced Lyell was right after seeing earthquakes and volcanoes, and finding fossils of seashells on top of high mountains. He started to believe that the world and the living things in it were indeed very, very old and that they could and did change over time.

DARWIN THE COLLECTOR

Everywhere he went, Darwin collected samples of the plants, animals and fossils he saw, and he made lots of long, careful notes. These collections and records were to provide the clues he needed to develop his remarkable theory after he returned to England in 1836. He collected over 1,500 species and almost 4,000 other specimens. He preserved the animal samples in jars of wine. He spent the next 20 years analysing his specimens and working on his theory, knowing that he would need to be able to back up his theory with solid evidence.

DARWIN'S FINCHES

Darwin collected some songbirds from a group of islands called the Galápagos Islands. On his return, he discovered that although the birds had very different beaks, they were all closely related species of finches. Finches on different islands had different beak shapes in order to eat different foods that were available. So, for example, some had stout beaks for eating seeds and others had narrow beaks for catching insects. Darwin realised that these birds were descendants of a single species that had adapted to eat the various foods available after they moved to different islands, and had developed into 13 different species. This proved to him that over time species adapt to their particular habitats.

ON THE ORIGIN OF SPECIES

Darwin needed time to be sure of his evidence, but the other reason he held back from publishing his theory of evolution for so long was that he knew the uproar it would cause. He was right to be nervous!

GOING PUBLIC

Darwin was spurred into action in 1858, when he received a letter from a young naturalist named Alfred Russel Wallace. Wallace had made two long voyages, collecting specimens and studying nature, and his letter outlined a theory of evolution almost identical to Darwin's own.

So, Darwin arranged for the two of them to present their theory at an important gathering of scientists. One reason why Darwin became better known for the theory than Wallace is because when his book, *On the Origin of Species*, came out in 1859, it instantly made Darwin famous.

KEY IDEAS

These are the key ideas Darwin wrote about in *On the Origin of Species*:

▶ Over time, some species are created and some die out. While species exist they can change. This is evolution.

▶ All living things are related and evolved have in different ways from a common ancestor.

▶ Some members of a species can gradually change until they become a new species.

▶ Evolution is a very, very slow process that happens after many small changes occur within a species over generations.

▶ Evolutionary change happens because of variation between individuals in a species, which gives some individuals and their offspring a better chance of survival.

When On the Origin of Species *published in 1859, it sold out on the first day and attracted enormous attention.*

ANGER AND OUTRAGE

Many people in Britain were horrified by Darwin's *On the Origin of Species*, because it challenged the Christian belief that God created life on Earth. The book was reviewed, attacked and criticised by a range of people, including some of Darwin's fellow scientists. It was famously and angrily attacked by powerful figures such as Samuel Wilberforce, bishop of Oxford. Fortunately, Darwin's friend and fellow scientist Thomas Henry Huxley, publically supported Darwin's theory and gave the book favourable reviews. Darwin was an excellent scientist, but not such an impressive public speaker, whereas Huxley had the ability to defend and promote Darwin's views to the world.

Scientists continued to argue about which parts of Darwin's theory were right and which were wrong for many years, but as the evidence mounted up it became clear that Darwin was basically right. And although Darwin's theory has been tweaked and expanded over time, it is now generally accepted as the best evidence-based explanation for the amazing diversity of life on Earth.

DARWIN'S BULLDOG

Huxley's dogged and determined defence of Darwin's On the Origin of Species *earned him the nickname 'Darwin's Bulldog'.*

Thomas Henry Huxley was an important scientist and had travelled to Australia and New Guinea, where he had collected and studied sea animals. He met Charles Darwin in around 1856 and was won over by his theory of evolution by natural selection. In 1863, Huxley published his own book on evolution, focusing on the evolution of humans and apes from common ancestors.

LOOKING AT THE EVIDENCE

For most of Earth's history, there was no one about to write down what was happening or to keep records of which plants and animals existed. Fossils are pretty much the only clues we have about which plants and animals lived long ago and to help us piece together the history of the Earth. Fossil evidence clearly shows that life is old and has changed over time.

THE FOSSIL RECORD

One of the fossils Darwin had found was of a giant armoured animal, called a glyptodont, which he realised looked like the smaller armadillos he had seen in South America. This was evidence of a modern species that had evolved from an older one. By comparing fossils to modern plants and animals, scientists could tell which living things were related and therefore how each of them evolved and from what. Fossils show how much, or how little, organisms have changed over time. The fossil record shows that since life on Earth began about 3.5 billion years ago, many species have become extinct.

In the nineteenth century, Mary Ann Mantell found a tooth, which turned out to be the tooth of a dinosaur, Iguanodon, the first dinosaur fossil in the world ever to be identified.

FIRST FOSSIL

The first fossil was identified in the seventeenth century, when Danish scientist Nicholas Steno dissected a shark and noticed that its teeth looked exactly like 'tongue stones', triangular pieces of rock known since ancient times. Steno realised that the stones, in fact, came from the mouths of once-living sharks, but he had no idea how they could have turned to stone inside layers of rock.

HISTORY OF THE HORSE

One of the problems with the fossil record is that it contains gaps. Not all organisms fossilise well and others are destroyed by the movements of the Earth, or have simply not been discovered yet. The horse is one of the few animals for which we have a fairly complete evolutionary record. All the main stages of the evolution of the horse have been found in fossil form. They show that over 60 million years, the horse evolved from a dog-sized creature living in forests into a large animal up to 2 metres tall that lived on open plains. In the process, its feet, which once had several toes for walking across the forest floor, evolved into hooves for running over open country.

Fossil horse skeletons tell us that ancient horses were much smaller than the modern horses they have evolved into, and that they had three toes, rather than a single hoof, on each leg.

MARY ANNING: FOSSIL HUNTER

Famous fossil hunter Mary Anning was just 11 when she found the first ichthyosaur fossil skeleton. She lived on the coast of Dorset in the early 1800s and sold shells and other things she found on the beach to tourists. As well as finding the first complete fossil Ichthyosaurus, or 'fish-lizard', she found a giant sea reptile, a plesiosaur (swimming reptile), prehistoric fish and much more. She liked to hunt on the beach after a storm, because the wind, rain and waves made the cliffs crumble away to reveal fossils that had been buried in the rock.

HOW FOSSILS FORMED

Fossils are remains of plants and animals that lived millions of years ago and that are usually – but not always – preserved in rock. Most fossils are of individual body parts, such as shells or teeth, but sometimes people find complete plants or animal bodies. So exactly how do different fossils form and how do we find them?

TURNING INTO ROCK

The majority of fossils found are sea animals that had shells, such as the giant ancient sea snails we call ammonites. When an animal like this died and sank to the seabed, its soft body parts rotted away and the shell gradually became buried by layers of sediment (sand and mud). Over time, water seeped into the shell and minerals from the water replaced the minerals in the shell. The weight of sediment pressing down from above gradually made the minerals (and the sediment around the shell) turn to hard rock, in exactly the same shape as the original shell. This is how a sea creature became a fossil.

FINDING FOSSILS

Sometimes people find fossils deep in a mine or quarry, but most often fossils come near to the surface due to weathering and erosion. This is the way that wind, rain, rivers, seas and ice gradually wear away rocks at the Earth's surface and then wash or blow those bits of rock away. Over millions of years, weathering and erosion reveal fossils that were once far below the surface.

How a fossil is formed. This process takes hundreds of thousands of years!

TRACE FOSSILS

When a dinosaur walked in sand or mud and left a footprint, that mud sometimes got buried in layers of sediment that gradually turned to rock, leaving fossil footprints. Trace fossils, such as footprints, droppings or eggs, are remains that an ancient animal left behind. They are really useful because they can tell us things, such as how an animal lived and moved. Trace fossils are often the only evidence we have of some soft-bodied animals, as soft body parts rot away before they can turn into fossils.

TRAPPED IN TIME

Some fossils are of animals that got trapped in a substance, so they are actually the remains, rather than a fossil impression. Long ago, insects and spiders sometimes got stuck in resin – the sticky stuff that can ooze out of a tree's bark. As the resin dried and hardened, it became a clear rock called amber, perfectly preserving the animals inside. In California, USA, bones of ancient animals, such as sabre-toothed tigers, have been discovered in tar pits – pools of oil on land that perfectly preserved their bones. And fossils of woolly mammoths – giant elephant-like animals with hairy bodies and huge tusks – have been found preserved in ice in Siberia, after falling into icy waters and freezing to death thousands of years ago.

Some animals, such as frozen woolly mammoths, that last walked the Earth around 4,000 years ago, are so perfectly preserved that they still have clumps of hair intact.

15

ISLAND INDIVIDUALS

From giant Komodo dragons and huge hissing cockroaches to tiny rabbits and miniature snakes, some of the world's weirdest animals exist on islands. The reason for this is further evidence of the powers of evolution!

GALÁPAGOS TORTOISES

The giant tortoises that Darwin saw (and rode on!) in the Galápagos Islands are a case in point. The 19 islands of the Galápagos are the tips of volcanoes that began emerging from the ocean around 5 million years ago. The plants and animals on the islands today are descended from species that mainly arrived by sea or air. One explanation is that ancestors of today's giant tortoises (or their eggs) floated to one of the islands from the mainland. These tortoises evolved into the giant tortoises we see on Galápagos today. This can happen when an animal arrives on an island where it has no predators and it no longer needs to be able to hide.

ISLAND LIFE

Islands form in different ways, for example when sea levels rise and cut off a piece of land from a continent, or when an undersea volcano erupts and rises above the water level. Animals and plants get stuck on an island or end up there by accident. Animals that arrive on islands find very little competition and lots of empty habitats to live in. As populations grow, animals may evolve to specialise in different types of food or to live in different spaces, to avoid competition between each other.

Galápagos giant tortoises can weigh up to 250 kg and live for more than 100 years.

THE LEMURS OF MADAGASCAR

Madagascar is an island off the coast of Africa. Scientists believe that it broke off from the mainland about 165 million years ago and gradually shifted to its current location. Some species floated along with it, while others arrived later. Primates, such as monkeys and apes, never made it to Madagascar, so the lemurs that floated over to the island on logs and plants about 50 million years ago had no competition and they soon came to fill its rainforests. As lemur numbers increased, they evolved into different types of lemurs that specialised by living in different spaces within the forests and eating different foods. This helped them to avoid competing with each other over the same foods and habitats. Lemurs in other parts of the world died out because they faced predators that the lemurs of Madagascar didn't and they couldn't compete with other primates for food.

LOADS OF LEMURS!

Over 30 different species of lemur live in Madagascar today. They range in size from the tiny pygmy mouse lemur, which is about the size of your thumb, to the black and white indri lemur, which is about 70 cm long and can leap 10 metres between trees. Most lemurs live in trees, but the ring-tailed lemur spends more time on the ground. Different lemurs eat different things, too.

WHO'S THERE?

The aye-aye is an unusual lemur. At night, it taps dead trees and where they sound hollow the aye-aye listens out for insect grubs inside. Then, it rips the bark open using its long, powerful front teeth and fishes out the grub using its long, skinny middle finger.

For example, the bamboo lemur eats bamboo (no surprises there, then!), the aye-aye eats insects that live in tree bark and black lemurs feed on fruit, flowers and young leaves.

SAME PROBLEM, SAME SOLUTIONS

Animals that live in different parts of the world and are quite unrelated often evolve similar features if they live in similar habitats or have similar lifestyles. This is called convergent evolution. (To converge means to come from different directions and meet at the same point.) One of the reasons for convergent evolution is that there are a limited number of solutions to some problems and different species eventually end up with the same solutions to those challenges.

FISH ANTIFREEZE

If you're a fish and the waters you live in are icy cold, how do you survive? The Antarctic toothfish has adapted by evolving a kind of antifreeze that circulates in its blood and stops the growth of ice crystals, keeping the blood liquid. It's an amazing adaptation that allows these fish to survive in frozen oceans. It is such a good solution that at the other end of the Earth, Arctic cod also evolved to have antifreeze in their blood. By studying the fish, scientists know that the two species are unrelated and that they evolved separately. It's just an example of convergent evolution!

People use a type of antifreeze made from alcohol to stop the fluids in a car's motor from freezing during the winter. The antifreeze inside species of polar fish does the same sort of job but works a bit differently. Fish are lucky, though – they don't have to remember to top up with antifreeze regularly, so they won't get caught out like people often do!

ANT EATERS

Termites and ants live in large colonies. They are very aggressive if disturbed and you need to eat a lot of them to get the goodness you need to survive, so you wouldn't think many animals had adapted to eat these minibeasts. Wrong! Ant eaters found as far apart as Australia, Africa and America, such as the giant anteater and the pangolin, are not closely related, but they have evolved in similar ways to be able to feed on the tricky insects. Each have strong front legs and sharp hook-like claws for ripping open sun-baked mud nests. They also have tube-like snouts that house a long, sticky tongue for lapping up ants and termites from deep holes. These adaptations allow the giant anteater and the pangolin to eat a food that many other animals cannot or dare not eat!

The giant anteater of South America has long hair and the pangolin of Asia and Africa is covered with hard brown overlapping scales. Yet, they have both evolved similar solutions for catching ants – no teeth, a long sticky tongue, huge claws and a long, narrow skull.

PLANT POWER

Convergent evolution can be seen in the world of plants, too. Cacti survive happily in hot, dry American deserts because they have stems that can swell up and store water when there's a rare spell of rain. They also have sharp spines instead of leaves, to stop animals eating them to get at the water they contain. Although they are completely unrelated to cacti, the euphorbias of Africa developed the same features to cope with the hot, dry conditions there.

EVOLVING TOGETHER

Living things in our world are very closely connected, so it's no surprise that as different species evolved, some evolved together. They evolved to make use of each other in a way that helps both species out. This is called symbiosis, from the Greek word meaning 'living together'.

BEES AND FLOWERS

Bees and flowers are a great example of symbiotic evolution. Bees fly from plant to plant, collecting a sugary substance called nectar from the flowers, which they make into food. As they do so, some pollen from one flower rubs on to their hairy bodies. When they land on the next flower, some pollen rubs off and pollinates this next plant. It starts seeds developing inside the flower that can grow into new plants. Both the bees and the flowers behave in their own interests, but each gets something out of it, too. The bees get food and the flowering plants get to reproduce.

Flowers have bright petals and scents to attract bees and some even have lines, called honey guides, on their petals to lead bees to the nectar – and right past the pollen!

A SELFISH START

Evolving together isn't as cosy as it sounds. Scientists think that most symbiotic relationships began with one organism taking advantage of another, for example when one organism lives in or on and steals food from another. The organism being negatively impacted gradually evolves in order to gain something from the relationship, too.

ANEMONE AND CLOWNFISH

Clownfish and sea anemones are another perfect partnership. A clownfish's skin is covered in a special type of mucus that can fool a sea anemone into thinking the fish is just another part of itself. This allows the clownfish to hide safely among anemone tentacles without the anemone trying to sting it and stay safe from predators that dare not get too close to those long, stinging arms. Clownfish also get food from sea anemones. They eat leftovers of fish paralyzed by the tentacles and eaten by the anemone. In return, the clownfish keeps the anemone healthy by eating any rotten or damaged tentacles and many of the tiny animals that could damage the anemone.

The black stripes between the orange and white colours on a clownfish are different widths on different types of clownfish. Clownfish that live within bigger sea anemones have thicker, darker black stripes. This helps to camouflage the clownfish among the shadows of the moving tentacles.

BACTERIA AND US

We are part of a symbiotic relationship, too! As humans evolved, certain bacteria evolved along with us, to live in our gut. We need these bacteria and they need us. The bacteria help to break down the food we eat as it passes through our intestines. The bacteria get food to eat and somewhere safe to live. There is 1.4kg of bacteria in the average adult human gut — that's roughly the same weight as the human brain!

HOW DO SPECIES EVOLVE?

Further evidence for evolution came as scientific technology developed and scientists discovered exactly how traits and characteristics get passed on from parents to their offspring in genes. No not jeans — genes!

GENIUS GENES

Living things are made up of microscopic building blocks, called cells. Every cell contains pairs of chromosomes, which contain the genes. Genes are pieces of DNA inside each cell that tell the cell what to do and when to grow and divide. (If you must know, DNA stands for deoxyribonucleic acid — try saying that quickly!) Each gene is made up of a specific DNA sequence that contains the chemical instructions for a particular job or function in the body. Genes can make some cells become muscle cells and others become bone cells. They determine whether you have blue or green eyes or are short or tall.

DISCOVERING DNA

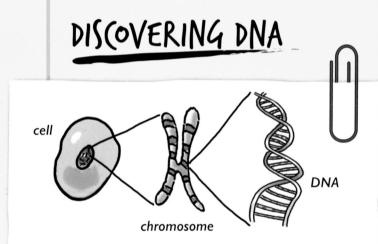

cell

chromosome

DNA

Inside each cell are chromosomes. Chromosomes contain long strands of genetic codes made up of DNA. A gene is a short section of DNA.

In the 1950s, scientists competed to solve the mystery of DNA structure. Rosalind Franklin and Maurice Wilkins studied DNA using X-rays. Franklin took an X-ray photograph which Wilkins took to scientists James Watson and Francis Crick, who used it to work out the 3D shape of DNA. Crick, Watson and Wilkins were awarded a Nobel Prize for their discovery but Franklin's contribution was only noted much later.

A UNIQUE CODE

Living things start out as a single cell, which is made from a combination of cell material from each parent. This new cell contains 23 pairs of chromosomes, half from the mother and the other half from the father, which is why offspring often look a lot like their parents. The genes, or DNA codes, in these 46 chromosomes arrange themselves in a new way, so the offspring ends up with a unique set that makes it slightly different to the rest of its species and even to its parents.

For offspring to grow, the new single cell divides into two, and those cells divide into two, and so on. Genes inside the cells guide the way the cells grow and develop, so some grow into skin cells and others into bone cells, for example. The different cells grow and arrange themselves to form different body parts, eye colour and so on, creating a brand-new, totally unique individual.

The fact that all living things have very similar DNA suggests that we all came from a common ancestor. Through evolution, little changes in this ancestor's DNA meant that different versions started to appear and evolve.

EVIDENCE FOR EVOLUTION

The discovery that all living things on Earth have DNA in their cells suggests that all life is related and came from the same beginnings. Scientists also compare the DNA of different species to find out how closely or distantly related they are. This helps them work out how genetic changes happened over time to make new species.

NATURAL SELECTION

If living things are all slightly different, then it stands to reason that some will be better equipped to survive in a particular environment than others. And because these individuals are more likely to live long enough to reproduce, they are the ones that will pass on their genes to future generations. This is natural selection – nature's way of selecting the best characteristics or features to help a species evolve and thus survive.

MUTATIONS

As we've seen, individuals in a species show a wide range of variation as a result of differences in their genes. Some of these differences occur because occasionally, when cells divide, the genes inside them don't copy properly and the DNA gets altered or damaged, causing a mutation. A mutation can be very minor, like slightly longer ears, or major, such as a missing leg. Most mutations make no difference to an organism, but once in a while a mutation comes along that gives an individual a better chance of survival.

FINDING FOSSILS

Darwin used the giraffe's long neck as an example of natural selection. Because of genetic variation, a few giraffes had longer necks than others. This allowed them to reach sources of food other giraffes could not reach. These giraffes were more likely to survive than shorter-necked giraffes that were competing with each other for shorter plants to eat. The long-necked giraffes would survive and their offspring would have a chance of inheriting a long neck, too. Over long periods, long-necked giraffes survived and flourished.

The giraffe's 2-metre long neck is a result of natural selection. It helps it reach high branches and spot danger; they can see a lion a kilometre away!

SURVIVAL OF THE FITTEST

It's a jungle out there – well, not literally, but most living things have to struggle to survive. They have to compete with other living things for food and shelter and must constantly be on the lookout for dangers, such as the hungry jaws of a predator. Animals born with slight genetic variations that help them survive, are more likely to be the ones in their species that live long enough to reproduce.

For example, imagine long ago a tiger was born with a mutated gene that gave it some stripes. The stripes helped it to blend into the tall grasses in the habitat where it lived. This helped it to sneak up on prey, such as deer, so it rarely went hungry. When it reproduced, it passed on the mutated gene to its offspring and they passed it on to their offspring. Tigers without stripes caught fewer prey, so often went without food and eventually died out. Gradually, all tigers evolved to have the same mutated gene and similar stripes. Understanding how natural selection works, along with evidence from fossils, helps us to understand how living things evolved from common ancestors in the past.

This is an example of how natural selection works.

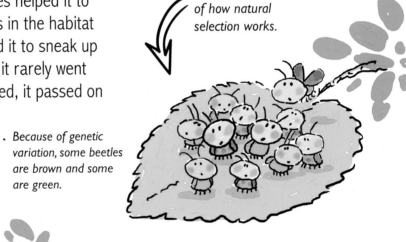

1. *Because of genetic variation, some beetles are brown and some are green.*

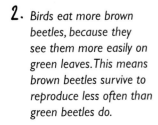

2. *Birds eat more brown beetles, because they see them more easily on green leaves. This means brown beetles survive to reproduce less often than green beetles do.*

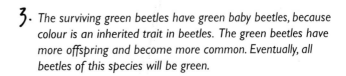

3. *The surviving green beetles have green baby beetles, because colour is an inherited trait in beetles. The green beetles have more offspring and become more common. Eventually, all beetles of this species will be green.*

ANIMALS ONTO LAND

The first living things on Earth were single-celled organisms, such as the bacteria that once lived in volcanic hot springs. By 1,000 million years ago there were also early water plants called algae. In the sea, single-celled organisms began to grow together in clusters, eventually forming the first multi-cellular animals, such as jellyfish and worms. Some of these evolved into shelled animals, such as ammonites. But how and when did animal life leave the water?

ANIMALS ON LAND

Arthropods were the first animals on land. After algae spread from water onto land, the first true plants developed, with leaves that captured sunlight and allowed them to make their own food. Insects evolved from ancient sea worms to take advantage of this new food supply. The first to crawl out of the sea were probably early forms of millipede. Soon other land invertebrates (animals without backbones) developed, such as giant scorpions, spiders and centipedes.

THE FIRST FISH

The earliest vertebrates (animals with backbones) were the fish that appeared around 550 million years ago. The first fish evolved backbones to support the

muscles and long body that helped them swim quickly through water. By about 350 million years ago, some fish developed larger fins with bones that they could use for walking on the seabed. This also allowed those animals to crawl onto land and lay their eggs there, where the eggs and hatchlings were safer from all the predators that had evolved to eat them in the water.

You might think flies are a nuisance now, but they are nothing compared to the giant dragonflies of prehistoric times. They were the same size as seagulls!

FROM FISH TO FROGS!

Early amphibians, which evolved into the toads, frogs, and later all other land vertebrates alive today, evolved from fish that could crawl onto land. Gradually, the fins evolved into legs and the amphibians developed lungs for breathing on land. Fossils of early amphibians, such as Ichthyostega, show that they were related to fish: they had a head and tail like a fish, but legs for walking in shallow water. Like amphibians today, early amphibians lived a double life — living partly on land and partly in the water, where they laid eggs and their young started to develop.

REPTILES – LIVING ON LAND

Most amphibians stayed by the water, but some evolved into reptiles that could live on land all the time, where they could take advantage of the food, as well as limited predators and competition. To do this, they evolved a skin that acts as a watertight barrier to stop them drying out and a new kind of egg. Reptile eggs contain their own water and food supply and are surrounded by a leathery or hard shell to stop the young inside from drying out, so eggs could be laid on dry land.

FEARSOME REPTILES

The first reptiles were small, lizard-sized animals with amphibian-like skulls. But reptiles gradually evolved into different species such as tortoises, snakes and crocodiles, some of which became much larger. The biggest crocodile was 15 metres long!

Fossils of the biggest snake ever found suggest it was longer than a bus and heavier than a car!

DINOSAURS TO BIRDS

It may be hard to believe that the budgie sitting in your grandpa's sitting room is distantly related to an ancient group of deadly carnivores, but it's true! Evidence from fossils has shown that birds evolved from a group of small meat-eating theropod dinosaurs, such as the Velociraptor.

AGE OF THE DINOSAURS

Dinosaurs were a new group of reptiles that evolved about 230 million years ago. There were hundreds of different types. Diplodocus was a gentle giant that used its incredibly long neck to eat leaves from treetops, while Ankylosaurus had a sharp, club-shaped tail to fight off predators. The fearsome Tyrannosaurus rex had an alarming set of huge, saw-edged teeth. Theropod dinosaurs were flesh-eating predators that walked on two legs. Scientists studying fossil theropods discovered many similarities between these dinosaurs and birds that evolved later. Both have similar-shaped hollow bones, laid similar-looking eggs and fossils have been found of theropods that died sitting on their nests, show that they shared nesting behaviours, too!

DISCOVERING DINOSAURS

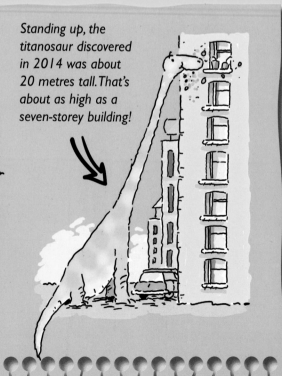

Standing up, the titanosaur discovered in 2014 was about 20 metres tall. That's about as high as a seven-storey building!

Amazing new dinosaur fossils are still being discovered. In 2014, fossils of possibly the biggest dinosaur that ever walked the Earth were found in the desert in Patagonia, Argentina. Based on the size of the thigh bones – which are taller than an average man – this titanosaur was about 40 metres long from its head to the tip of its tail.

ARCHAEOPTERYX

Fossils of Archaeopteryx, a magpie-sized animal with features of both theropods and birds that lived 150 million years ago, were discovered in 1861. Biologist Thomas Henry Huxley had predicted that an animal like Archaeopteryx must have existed even before its fossil was found, and in 1868 he showed that Archaeopteryx was a missing stage in evolution between birds and reptiles. Like theropods, Archaeopteryx had jaw bones and teeth and a long, lizard-like tail, but like birds it had feathers on its arms that it could use to fly and clawed toes that helped it perch on branches in trees.

A SLOW PROCESS

As in most cases of evolution, birds evolved very gradually through different stages. Take feathers, for example. Feathers are thought to have evolved from the scales that covered dinosaur skin. When theropods evolved the first feathers, they were short and hair-like and were probably used to keep the dinosaurs warm. Later, some theropods had longer feathers, which may have evolved to spread over eggs to keep them warm or for displaying to other dinosaurs. One example for this is the modern peacock's bright plumage. Gradually, as this group of small, agile, two-legged dinosaurs evolved into birds, the feathers changed again and again and the arms grew longer until they evolved into feathered wings that could fly. Over the last 65 million years, these early birds diversified into the great variety of birds that are alive today.

Many half-bird, half-dinosaur fossils have been found since Archaeopteryx. They show how large theropods evolved to be smaller, so they could live and feed in trees and avoid competing with the giant dinosaurs on land. One of the dinosaurs most closely related to birds was the Microraptor. It couldn't fly but probably used its four wings to glide from tree to tree.

29

MAMMALS AND US

While one branch of reptiles evolved into birds and modern reptiles, another evolved into mammals. Around 200 million years ago, the main mammals were small insect-eaters that lived in forests, rather like the shrews you might see today.

EARLY MAMMALS

Instead of laying eggs like reptiles, early mammals gave birth to live young that fed on their mother's milk, which meant their babies were more likely to survive their first months. Another difference was that mammals evolved hair from the reptile's scales, just as birds had evolved feathers, to keep them warm. Gradually, a range of distinct mammals evolved to occupy other spaces and roles in different habitats. Large, hoofed mammals, such as deer and rhinos, evolved to graze on plants, while carnivorous mammals, such as dogs, cats and bears, evolved to stalk prey. Whales are mammals whose ancestors returned to the sea around 50 million years ago and whose legs evolved into flippers ideally suited to swimming fast. Around 30 million years ago, a huge variety of new species of mammals developed, including horses, anteaters and primates (monkeys, apes and humans).

MAMMALS TAKE FLIGHT

Bats developed from small mammals that jumped from tree to tree to catch flying insect prey. Those with longer fingers with skin between them could stay in the air longer, so they and their ancestors caught more food and survived better than those with shorter fingers. Gradually, all bats evolved to be born with wings.

Longer fingers with skin between them helped early bats catch food, so over many generations bat fingers gradually became longer and the skin between them wider. Eventually, they developed into wings that the bats could use to swoop through the air to chase and catch flying insects.

PRIMATES

The oldest primate fossils date from about 60 million years ago. These suggest that early primates were about the size of squirrels, had fairly good eyesight and hands and feet with pads and claws for climbing trees. Gradually, larger primates evolved. These early monkeys and apes had bigger brains and fingers that could pick things up. Around 7 to 8 million years ago, the apes evolved into different types, such as gibbons, gorillas and chimpanzees, and one branch evolved into our early human ancestors!

HUMANKIND

The first human-like creatures, or hominids, walked on two legs, just like us. It is thought hominids evolved this way to help them move across open ground when the climate became too dry for forests to thrive. Becoming bipedal like this resulted in other advantages, too. These primates had their hands free to do other things, such as learn to make tools, and they could see predators and prey more easily. Over time, there were many different species of hominids, but after the modern human species, Homo sapiens, had evolved, it killed off all the others.

LUCY

'Lucy' is the nickname of a fossil discovered in 1974 of perhaps the world's most famous female hominid. Lucy lived around 3.2 million years ago and, like a chimpanzee, she was just over a metre tall and had a small brain, long, dangly arms, short legs and a large belly. However, the knee and pelvis fossil bones showed she also walked upright on two legs, like us.

DNA studies show humans and chimpanzees shared a common ancestor that lived in Africa 7–8 million years ago and that chimpanzees are our closest relatives, in terms of evolution. We share about 98 per cent of our DNA with them – even if most of us look quite different on the surface.

EXTINCTIONS

As some species evolve, others can die out. When all of the last members of a species have gone, we say that the species is extinct. Some extinctions happen very slowly or gradually, but others can happen quite suddenly.

SPEEDY DEATH OF THE DINOSAURS

About 66 million years ago, in the area that is now Mexico, a huge asteroid hit the planet. The impact caused tsunamis across the oceans, powerful earthquakes and fires. It threw up a thick blanket of dust so vast that it shaded Earth from sunlight. Plants could no longer make their food and the climate changed. With fewer plants, plant-eating dinosaurs died out, meaning there were fewer animals for carnivorous (flesh-eating) dinosaurs to eat. Experts believe that the impact of the asteroid wiped out the dinosaurs and every other land animal that weighed more than about 25 kilograms. In fact, around 80 per cent of the species alive on Earth at the time quickly became extinct.

GOOD FOR US

One animal's loss is another animal's gain... The mass extinction was bad news for the Tyrannosaurus rex and its kind, but good news for other animals. Birds, lizards and snakes flourished because they had more space, feeding opportunities and fewer predators. For the same reason, small early mammals gradually evolved into a rich variety of different types, too.

It's a possibility that if that asteroid hadn't smashed into Earth 66 million years ago, humans might not be here and dinosaurs could still be roaming the planet!

SLOW RISE OF HOMO SAPIENS

We human beings are what's left after a much slower type of extinction. Even 100,000 years ago, there were still several closely related hominids on Earth and until 25,000 years ago homo sapiens (that's us) lived alongside strong, stocky Neanderthals. These other hominids gradually became extinct, leaving us as the sole humans on Earth. Experts think what helped homo sapiens survive when other species died out was our cleverness and adaptability. Homo sapiens was better at finding ways to keep warm when the climate cooled down, or keep cool when it warmed up. Other hominid species had big brains, too, but homo sapiens could communicate and plan, and learned to make fires and decent shelters. Homo sapiens also made increasingly advanced tools and weapons, which meant they could outcompete other hominids for food and were more likely to win in a fight.

OUTCOMPETED AND OUTNUMBERED

A good example of the gradual extinction of a species is homo erectus. Long ago, the homo erectus species of hominids left Africa and gradually spread across Asia. That is, until homo sapiens also left Africa and reached Asia. Over a period of at least 40,000 years, and probably through a combination of climate change and the effects of being out-competed for scarce food by the spread of homo sapiens, homo erectus gradually died out. By 30,000 years ago, it was extinct.

Experts think that one reason earlier hominid species became extinct is that while homo sapiens made increasingly clever tools and weapons, such as spears, species such as homo erectus went on making the same sort of axe for many years!

EXTREME EVOLUTION

A shark's hammer-shaped head. A fennec fox's huge ears. A chimp's amazing ability to use tools. These astounding adaptations are body features or ways of behaving that evolved to help plants and animals to survive, reproduce or find food in different environments or situations. Some of evolution's solutions are pretty strange and extreme!

PLANT DEFENCES

Some acacia trees in Africa have evolved features that encourage ants to become their bodyguards! Acacia trees have long and very sharp thorns to deter large animals from eating their leaves and twigs. The thorns are also hollow. Ants bite a small hole in these thorns to build nests where they raise their young. The acacia also produces nectar that provides the ants with food. If any other type of animal climbs or lands on the tree, the ants swarm out and attack it to protect their homes. Of course, this also protects the tree from being munched and gives it a chance to grow bigger and make seeds.

THAT STINGS!

Even ordinary plants have some amazing adaptations. The hairs on a stinging nettle are tiny hollow tubes. When an animal brushes against the leaves, the tips of the hairs break off to leave a sharp point that injects the animal's skin with a stinging liquid. Unsurprisingly, this stops most animals grazing on the plant's leaves!

The acacia tree has taken evolution to the extreme. It 'employs' ants as bodyguards that will protect acacia trees with their lives!

CLEVER CAMOUFLAGE

Some animals are masters of disguise. They have evolved patterns, colours or behaviours that help them to hide. A polar bear's white fur helps it to sneak up on seals on the ice. A grasshopper's green body hides it against leaves from hungry predators. Stick insects are long-bodied insects that look like twigs. Some even have flaps on their legs and stomachs that look like dried leaves. They can remain incredibly still for a long time or sway to mimic the way branches move in the wind. This helps them hide amongst the branches of trees from predators, such as birds.

MOULDY SLOTH?

In the forests of South America, the three-toed sloth has evolved an incredible symbiotic relationship with moths and algae! Every week, the sloth leaves the safety of the treetops to go to the toilet on the forest floor. Why risk being eaten by jaguars and other predators? Because moths lay eggs in the sloth's dung pile and moth larvae live in it while they grow. As adults, the moths fly up into the trees to live in the sloth's fur. The moths add nutrients to the fur, which algae can feed on. The algae make the sloth's fur look green for camouflage and sloths eat the algae to supplement their diet of leaves.

When a sloth grooms itself, it moves its fingers very slowly so it doesn't disturb the moths living in its fur. If it groomed too roughly, over a hundred moths could fly out!

GETTING FOOD AND WATER

Most of us can be pretty devious and adaptable when we're hungry. What lengths have you gone to in order to reach the treats stashed in a high cupboard or to persuade your parents that pizza and chips is a healthy option for dinner? Over time, some plants and animals have evolved some extreme ways of getting their grub, too!

CAGE OF DEATH

The venus flytrap lives in habitats which are low on nutrients. It has evolved to get extra nutrients by devouring insects and other small animals. To do this, its leaves are adapted as deadly traps. Its green leaves are red on the inside to attract insects to feed on nectar in the leaf. The leaves also have spikes on the end and can open and close like jaws. When an insect crawls onto hairs on the surface of a leaf, the leaf snaps shut and the spikes form a cage. This traps and squashes the insect while the plant releases special substances called enzymes that break the prey's body down into tiny pieces that it can absorb. Yum!

A HAMMER FOR A HEAD?

As its name suggests, the hammerhead shark has a head shaped like a hammer. Its eyes are spread wide apart, on each end of the 'hammer', and this helps the shark to judge water depth and distance better than many other sharks. This helps it catch its dinner more easily.

The venus flytrap has inspired many horror films about dangerous, man-eating plants, but thankfully it usually only catches insects and the occasional frog in its fast-moving traps…

TOOL USE

Humans may have invented can openers and apple corers, but we aren't the only animals that have evolved tool-making skills to help them get food. Chimpanzees have developed several tools to get their food and drink. They crunch up soft leaves and use them like sponges to soak up and drink water from spaces that are hard to reach. They break, bite and twist twigs to a particular shape, length and thickness and then poke them into holes in tree trunks to scoop out termites and ants, which they quickly wipe into their mouths before the bugs can bite. Chimps also use stick tools to scoop honey from bee nests to avoid getting stung.

CRACKING CROWS!

Crows know some smart tricks. They drop stones into containers of water to raise the level of the liquid so they can reach inside to drink it. Like chimps, some clever crows also use sticks to get bugs out from trees, and others drop walnuts onto roads so that cars drive over the nuts and break them open.

Some crows in Japan not only know the best way to crack tough nuts, they understand road safety as well. They drop nuts on pedestrian crossings and wait until the lights turn red to collect the nuts cracked for them by passing cars!

KEEPING COOL OR WARM

Like most large animals, we wouldn't last long in icy polar regions or in the stifling heat of a sandy desert without all the special gear used by explorers. The animals that do live in those extreme environments have evolved special features and behaviours that help them survive.

HOT, HOT, HOT!

The fennec fox is the smallest of all foxes, but has the biggest ears: 15 centimetres might not sound that long, but they are massive in proportion to its head. They might look slightly surreal, but in the hot, sandy deserts of North Africa where it lives, those long ears help to keep this fox cool. Each ear contains more blood vessels per square centimetre than any other part of its body. These blood vessels are just below the surface of the skin so as blood passes through them, heat radiates out of the blood, reducing the fox's overall body temperature. Pretty clever! Fennec foxes also have long hair that shades them from the hot sun during the day and thick fur on the bottom of their feet that protects them from the hot sand.

Unlike the fennec fox, which has large ears to lose heat to keep it cool, its distant cousin the Arctic fox has short, rounded ears that reduce heat loss and help it to survive in its icy habitat. These two foxes are evolved for their particular habitats and would not survive long if they swapped places!

LIFE IN THE FREEZER

While the fennec fox is adapted to survive in burning hot temperatures of the desert, another fox — the Arctic fox — is perfectly evolved for life in the frozen Arctic. In winter, the Arctic fox is covered in thick white fur that camouflages it against the snow while it hunts rodents and birds, but which is also the warmest of all mammal fur. Its dense, woolly coat helps this species survive at temperatures of -50°C. In summer, this fox sheds some of its fur to keep cooler and its coat turns brown so that it is camouflaged against the rocks when the snow melts!

SSS...SNAKE

Sidewinders live in hot deserts, and these smallish rattlesnakes got their name from the peculiar way they move. To avoid dragging the whole of their long belly over the burning hot sand when moving, they loop and raise their body in S-shaped curves so that just two short sections of it touch the sand at any one time. They push against these points to move sideways. When not moving, the snakes burrow down under the surface sand or dive into the nearest animal burrow for shade.

As a sidewinder snake moves, it leaves a series of S-shaped marks in the sand. The sidewinder travels so quickly over deserts using its curious side-winding technique that it can catch mice, rats, lizards and sometimes birds to eat.

HAVING YOUNG

All living things strive to reproduce and have young. If they didn't, their species would soon die out. Some organisms have extraordinary adaptations or tactics to make sure they grow into adults and have young of their own. (A word of caution – if you're eating, we'd suggest finishing your meal before you continue to read this page!)

INVASION OF THE BODY SNATCHERS

To achieve its lifecycle, the green-banded broodsac flatworm invades first a snail and later a bird! When snails graze on grass, they may swallow flatworm eggs. Larvae hatch out of the eggs to live and grow inside the snails. Later, they burrow out of the snail's gut and swim to its eye stalks. Here, they gather together, swell in size and change colour. They make the snail's eye stalks pulsate with colour, so they look like caterpillars that birds prey on. Their presence also affects the snail's ability to detect light and dark, so that rather than hiding in the shade, it wanders into the open. This means birds soon see and devour it – along with the flatworms.

Disco snail! The bright colours and movement of the broodsac larvae show through the thin skin of a snail's swollen eye stalks and quickly attract the attention of passing birds. This usually ends with a bird eating the entire snail or, at the very least, its eye stalks.

Adult flatworms live and feed in the bird's gut and the cycle begins again when their eggs are released in bird poop and land on grass where unsuspecting snails graze.

LION LEADERS

The broodsac flatworm is an example of a physical adaption that has evolved to help a species survive. Some animals have evolved behaviours that help them to reproduce and pass on their genes. Each pride of lions has a male leader who is also the father of all the cubs in the pack.

If a new male from outside the group kills the leader and takes over the pride, he kills all the cubs. He does this because he wants to have cubs of his own and killing cubs ensures that the females are ready to have more babies again sooner. It also prevents the risk those infant males might kill him when they grow up.

CUCKOO CARERS

The female cuckoo has evolved in a way to ensure her young hatch and develop safely, while leaving herself free to lay more eggs. She lays a single egg among the eggs of another bird's nest. The babysitting bird unwittingly sits on the egg to keep it warm and when it hatches, she feeds the cuckoo chick as if it were her own.

To make sure it gets enough food, as soon as a cuckoo chick has hatched it pushes the other chicks out of the nest, so that its unsuspecting foster parents can spend all their time feeding it instead of their own young.

EVOLUTION IN ACTION

Evolution usually happens over hundreds or thousands of years, so it is far too slow a process for us to see. However, scientists are making new discoveries every day and studying some examples of evolution that are happening in front of our very eyes!

ANTIBIOTIC RESISTANT BACTERIA

Antibiotics are medicines that cure diseases by destroying the microscopic bacteria that cause them. However, in the last few decades scientists have noticed that many types of bacteria have evolved resistance to antibiotics and can no longer be killed by them. This is mainly because people haven't been using antibiotics properly. For example, taking them for things they cannot treat, such as viral infections. Or failing to complete a full course of antibiotics, so only some but not all of the bacteria are wiped out. When antibiotics kill weak bacteria but fail to destroy individual bacteria that carry a gene which helps them to survive, those more resistant bacteria reproduce, creating more bacteria that are resistant to the antibiotic. They and their descendants reproduce so rapidly that it can take just a few years for whole new types of antibiotic resistant bacteria to emerge.

Bacteria that are resistant to antibiotic medicines are very difficult to get rid of and that is bad news for us!

BAD NEWS BACTERIA

Everyone can all help to tackle the evolution of antibiotic resistant bacteria.

- Only use antibiotics when they are prescribed by a doctor.
- Complete the full treatment course, even if you feel better sooner.
- Never share antibiotics with other people or use leftover prescriptions.

42

ARMOUR-PLATED FISH

Evolution can be seen in action in bigger organisms, too. In the 1960s, the tiny stickleback fish living in Washington Lake in America did not have bony plates over their body, as some of their relatives living in other waters did. The water in their lake was so murky that they were hidden from predators and didn't need that adaptation to protect them. But after the lake was cleaned up and the water became clear, the sticklebacks rapidly evolved. Within decades, many of the fish had developed bony plates from head to tail.

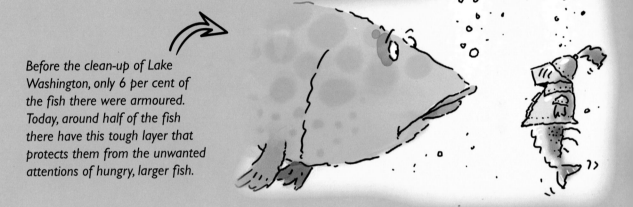

Before the clean-up of Lake Washington, only 6 per cent of the fish there were armoured. Today, around half of the fish there have this tough layer that protects them from the unwanted attentions of hungry, larger fish.

GROWING GUPPIES

In 2009, researchers did an experiment with guppies in Trinidad to see how fast they could evolve. Guppies are a species of fish that mature and reproduce quickly – there can be three generations of guppies per year. Researchers moved some guppies from a river where there were many predators, to one where there were none. When they returned 10 years later, the fish had evolved. In the old river, baby fish became adults quickly when they were still small because otherwise they would probably have been killed before they had a chance to reproduce. In the new river, the guppies had larger and fewer offspring because the young could grow up safely at a more leisurely pace!

RETURN OF THE PESTS

People across the world use chemicals to kill weeds, insects, rodents and other pests, but these poisons are not working as well as they used to. Over time, the pests are fighting back – they are developing the ability to resist the chemicals. This really is evolution in action!

ATTACKED AND ADAPTED

Farmers and gardeners spray pesticides on crops to kill insects that damage fruits and vegetables. They also use herbicides to kill weeds that may compete with the crops. Every time chemicals are sprayed on land to kill weeds or bugs, a few individuals survive because they are naturally resistant to the poisons. These survivors reproduce and create a new generation of pests that are poison-resistant. Then that generation produces another generation that is even more resistant. (Insects are quicker to develop resistance because they reproduce rapidly and in large numbers!) Eventually, the chemical poisons don't work on any of the weeds or bugs they are targeting.

RISE OF THE SUPER RATS

Rats carry diseases and can damage homes and public property, so around 50 years ago people started to put down strong poisons to get rid of them. Over generations, rats have developed a resistance that allows them to survive these pest control poisons.

In countries across the world, rats are becoming so resistant to the common poisons people put down to get rid of them, that they have been dubbed 'super rats'.

MAKING MATTERS WORSE

Pesticides are the world's most popular way to kill pests, but misuse is speeding up the evolution of resistant pests. If one dose of these chemicals doesn't work, then we spray more or use a stronger dose of the stuff. This often means that the pests that can survive the stronger doses thrive, reproduce and spread more rapidly because the weaker ones die more quickly. Without other pests to compete with them for food and space to live, resistant pests soon outnumber the ones we can control and the more sprays that are used, the more pests there are!

BACK TO NATURE

Some people prefer to use more natural methods of pest control. One way to do this is to encourage the spread of a pest's natural enemies or to grow plants among your crops that ward off bugs. For example, some gardeners grow flowering plants that encourage ladybirds, because ladybirds eat garden pests, called aphids. Also, planting thyme herbs in your cabbage patch should keep cabbage white butterflies away.

Farmers and gardeners also use so-called 'trap crops' to stop bugs attacking their fruit and vegetables. A trap crop is a plant that attracts insects away from the main crop. It's a bit like putting a bowl of ice cream near some raw brussel sprouts. Which would you choose?

PARASITES AND ALLERGIES

Scientists today are also studying the evolution of parasites and their connection with allergies, such as asthma and hay fever, which more and more people suffer from today. A parasite is a creature that lives off another living thing and uses their body to survive. Some parasites are so well-adapted to using humans as hosts, that when they are removed there may be surprising results!

PARASITE PESTS

Parasites evolved to live off other living things and usually harm or irritate their hosts. For example, head lice are perfectly adapted to climbing and gripping onto human hair and to sucking blood from the scalp. They get food and shelter but all their human victim gets is an itchy scalp! However, scientists have noticed that over the past 40 years as many developed countries have got rid of lots of the parasites, the number of people who have allergies has increased. In developing countries, where many people still have a variety of parasites, allergies are rare. Some scientists believe that these two things – allergies and parasites – are connected.

Gut worms, head lice and other parasites have a very high yuck factor, but almost every animal on Earth has evolved with its own set of parasites – and humans are no exception.

SENDING PARASITES PACKING

A parasite and its host may gradually evolve together. Parasites evolve ways to live in or on their hosts and use the hosts for food. Over time, hosts may develop ways of getting rid of or protecting themselves from parasites. For example, humans purify water before they drink it and can take medicines to destroy tapeworms in their stomachs.

FRIEND OR FOE?

Allergies are when the body's immune system, which evolved to defend us against things like germs, reacts badly to something that's usually harmless, such as dust or pollen. Some experts believe that over millions of years of evolving together, parasites such as the worms that can live in our guts, developed ways to dampen down their host's immune responses to stop it attacking them. When people get rid of all the gut worms and other parasites, their immune system can become unbalanced and they may get allergies. Another idea is that our immune system has evolved to need the early challenges that parasites give it in order to develop properly and attack other body invaders, such as bacteria. If it doesn't get the work-out that parasites give it to make it strong and efficient, maybe it can't help us to avoid allergies and other immune system disorders in later life.

GUT WORMS AND ASTHMA

Scientists are doing experiments to see how we and parasites evolved together. In a village in the countryside in Vietnam, many children were infected with hookworm and other parasitic worms, but rates of asthma and other allergies were low. After doctors gave the children treatment to clear their body of worms, this led to an increase in dust mite allergies.

Don't worry — no one is suggesting we should return to an unhygienic, parasite-filled environment. The hope is that by studying parasites, scientists can come up with new treatments which work in the same way as organisms like worms, by dampening down or rebalancing the immune system so that the body does not overreact to things such as pollen or dust.

ARTIFICIAL SELECTION

What do sweetcorn, a cow and a labradoodle all have in common? They were all created by humans! They exist because of artificial selection. In natural selection, plants and animals evolve in response to things in the natural world. In artificial selection, humans control which organisms survive and reproduce. We breed animals and plants for particular traits and we can even create whole new species!

A CORNY TALE

The story of how juicy, delicious sweetcorn came to exist is a classic example of artificial selection. Long ago, the ancestors of sweetcorn plants were wild cereal or grass plants that grew short ears with only half a dozen tough seeds, or kernels. Then humans stepped in. They spotted that some plants had more and bigger seeds. They collected seeds from these plants and grew new plants using only those seeds. Generations of humans kept selecting and planting only seeds from plants that had ears with many large kernels. Gradually, over many years, we ended up with the sweetcorn we have today, which is up to 30 centimetres long and can have 500 or more tasty kernels!

Sweetcorn's tough and inedible ancestors might have broken your teeth – and there were no dentists around in those days!

It's all because of artificial selection that we can sit down to a plate of soft, juicy sweetcorn today.

48

DOMESTICATION

The ancestors of our docile, milk-yielding cattle were large, aggressive creatures called aurochs. At first, ancient people hunted these wild animals for food. Then, they started to keep them for meat and to use their skins for clothing. They selected and bred only the cows that produced the most milk and that were calmer and easier to handle. They avoided breeding animals that were more aggressive and made less milk. Over time, people have created cows that produce lots of milk, are gentle and are happy to do as a farmer tells them — most of the time! This is what we call domestication.

Getting milk in the past was a much more dangerous affair than it is today!

SELECTIVE BREEDING

Today's dogs were probably domesticated from grey wolves, and are now a distinct subspecies. Within the dog subspecies there are over 400 different breeds. To get different dog breeds, people selected animals with certain traits and characteristics and bred those animals together, over many generations. Dachshunds, Australian shepherds, Labrador retrievers and greyhounds all descended from the same ancestral wild dogs, but humans have used selective breeding to create different characteristics and features. Dachshunds have short legs and long bodies, greyhounds can run fast, Labrador retrievers are friendly and Australian shepherds are smart.

DID YOU KNOW?

Unfortunately, selective breeding to create pedigree dogs with exaggerated physical features, such as short flat faces, folded skin, short legs or very long floppy ears, has led to some problems. These features on some pedigree dog breeds may cause pain and suffering. For example, dogs with folded skin around their eyes may suffer eye problems.

49

CLONING

For a long time, people have been using artificial selection or selective breeding to produce the kinds of plants and animals they want. However, in recent years scientists have developed more dramatic ways to manipulate DNA to produce new organisms or species.

SEND IN THE CLONES

Clones are genetically identical individuals. Cloning sounds like something out of a sci-fi film, but it happens in nature, too. Plants, such as grasses and potatoes, and single-celled organisms, such as some bacteria, produce clones that are genetically identical to themselves. Identical human twins are also clones. In the last few decades, it has become possible to clone animals in a lab. In future, scientists could use the technique to clone individual cells and remove parts of genes that cause diseases or clone large numbers of organisms that can help us to make important drugs. We may even be able to use cloning to save endangered species – plants and animals in danger of becoming extinct.

DOLLY THE SHEEP

In 1996, Dolly the sheep became world-famous because she was the first ever cloned mammal. It took almost 300 attempts for scientists in Scotland to achieve this. Since then, scientists have cloned cows, pigs, rodents, cats, horses and monkeys.

It's pretty difficult to tell one sheep from another at the best of times, but in 1996 Dolly the sheep became the first actual clone – genetically identical to its 'parent' sheep in every way.

50

HOW CLONING WORKS

To clone, or make an exact copy of a plant or an animal, scientists first remove a cell from the organism. Then, they extract the DNA from that cell and insert it into another cell (that has had its DNA removed). When the new cell develops, it grows into an exact genetic copy of the original organism. Because all the genetic information in that new cell comes from only one parent cell, rather than a mix of two parent cells as usual, the DNA sequence of cloned organisms is exactly the same as that of the parent cell.

Some scientists say they might be able to clone some extinct animals such as woolly mammoths. They say they can take DNA from liquid blood samples taken from a frozen mammoth. Others say it isn't possible because DNA breaks down too much after death, but watch this space!

CLONING CONTROVERSIES

Cloning is a pretty controversial issue. People who support it point out that cloning can help to spread useful genes through large numbers of plants and animals very quickly. However, those who are against cloning say that there could be unknown effects and by taking away variation – the very stuff that powers evolution – we could be risking the health and diversity of the species. What do you think?

GENETIC MODIFICATION

Across the world, there is a shortage of food and many people don't have enough to eat. This is partly due to the rapidly rising population and partly because some countries have poor soils or lack water. To increase the amount of food we produce we could use conventional artificial selection, but this can be slow. Some scientists are doing it by genetic modification – moving DNA from one organism into another – to put evolution on fast forward!

HOW GM WORKS

Scientists have worked out how to cut the pieces of DNA for a particular gene from one organism and join them into a gap in the DNA of another organism. This gives the second organism (with the inserted genes) instructions for some new characteristics. For example, to make a crop herbicide-resistant, scientists find a plant that has a natural resistance to herbicide, identify which gene creates this resistance and cut it out. Then they insert this DNA into seeds of the crop, so that when they grow into adult plants, the herbicides farmers spray on fields only kill the weeds and not the crops.

Cutting and reinserting bits of DNA might sound straightforward, but even the simplest traits usually involve networks of many different genes so scientists often have to tweak one gene after another to get it right. This makes genetic modification a very complicated process!

52

NEW GM PLANTS

Scientists are using genetic modification to try to develop plants that have all sorts of useful characteristics. For example, to create crops that can grow in places where there is little water or where the soil is poor and to make plants that produce more fruit or vegetables per plant or that are resistant to pests. Scientists even try to alter plants in the hope of curing illnesses or other conditions. In some African and south-east Asian countries, people often have a vitamin A deficiency and this can lead to blindness in children. To make sure people get more of the vitamin A they need to combat this problem from their regular foods, scientists have genetically modified a sweet potato with increased levels of vitamin A.

Scientists are using genetic modification to produce new types of plants. They have even developed plants that glow in the dark when they need watering!

THE GM DEBATE

Some people are excited by **GM** technology and think it will help us produce enough food to feed the world. Others fear there could be unknown consequences and that it is best not to interfere with natural evolution like this. For example, adding certain genes to crops can make them resistant to herbicides, which is good because it reduces the amount of herbicides farmers need to use. However, some people are concerned that problems with this genetic modification could include the development of herbicide-resistant weeds or that eating **GM** foods could have a bad long-term effect on human health, although so far there is no evidence of this.

BIODIVERSITY MATTERS

The amazing biodiversity on our planet is the result of millions of years of evolution. This precious diversity is under threat because many plants and animals cannot adapt and evolve quickly enough to the changes humans are making to their habitats.

HABITAT DESTRUCTION

Habitat destruction is one of the biggest threats. People fill in wetlands, such as marshes, and cut down forests and grasslands to make space for farmland, golf courses, airports and other buildings. They clear trees to make furniture, paper and other products, too. As the global population grows, more and more habitats are lost in this way. Without a place to find food, shelter and have young, living things starve and fail to reproduce.

POLLUTION

Pollution happens when people release waste, poisons or other substances into the air, water and land. For example, when rain washes pesticides and other farm chemicals into streams and rivers or when power stations release gases into the air. Pollution affects wildlife in different ways. Chemicals in water can cause birth defects and deformities in frogs and illnesses in seals and polar bears that eat fish which have swallowed pollutants in the sea.

PANDA PROBLEMS

Problems also occur when habitats get broken up. The giant panda's bamboo forest habitat in China has been divided up into lots of smaller patches. Pandas only eat bamboo, so if plants die in their patch, they cannot easily get to another area with healthy bamboo and they may starve.

Breaking up habitats also stops some animals reproducing. Giant pandas live alone and only meet up to mate. If roads divide their habitat, fewer young are born.

INVASIVE SPECIES

Invasive species are plants and animals from one area that move to a new place and harm the local wildlife in some way. Some arrive accidentally, perhaps when they seek refuge in a vehicle that then travels abroad. Others arrive in new places as pets, for sport or for food. When invaders escape and breed in the wild they compete with native wildlife for resources such as food and space. They also thrive if there are few or no predators to keep their numbers down in the new area.

When an invasive species moves into a new area, some animals may be easy targets because they do not recognise them and have not evolved ways of evading these new predators.

GLOBAL GREED

When people take too many plants or animals from a population for food, this also threatens a species' survival. For example, ocean overfishing is when people take fish from the sea at rates too high for those species to reproduce and replace their numbers. In some areas, large fishing boats have wiped out around 90 per cent of large fish species.

CLIMATE CHANGE

Climate change could have a big impact in the future. Climate change is the way that gases released by burning fossil fuels, such as coal and oil in power stations, cars and other sources, causes a gradual rise in average temperatures across the world. The rising temperature is affecting global climates in different ways and having a variety of impacts. For example, when oceans get warmer, coral reefs die and many tropical fish and other animals lose their homes. Climate change could also help invasive species to spread, for example insects that live in warm places will be able to spread to places where it was once too cold for them to survive.

WHY DOES BIODIVERSITY MATTER?

When humans change or damage wildlife habitats, some species adapt to the new conditions quickly but others are driven to extinction faster than new species can evolve. The International Union for the Conservation of Nature believes one in five mammals, one in three amphibians and one in seven birds are extinct or globally threatened, and other species are at risk, too. Why does this loss of biodiversity matter?

THE WEB OF LIFE

We need a variety of living things to keep the natural world healthy, because we are all connected. Each species depends on the services provided by other species to ensure survival. When you hear people talk about a balanced ecosystem, this is what they mean. Take the case of bees, for example. Many plants need bees to pollinate their flowers so they can produce seeds and reproduce. Many animals, such as caterpillars and rabbits, rely on those plants for food and they, in turn, are vital food sources for other animals, such as birds and foxes. If one link in this web of life, such as the bees, is lost, then this would affect many other species.

Honeybees are dying, probably from a combination of factors, such as the effects of pesticides and pollution. This is a problem, because honeybees pollinate about eight out of ten plants across the world and a single bee can visit 5,000 flowers a day!

RACOONS RACE AHEAD

Racoons have evolved ways of behaving that help them to quickly adapt to living in new types of habitats. Their natural habitat is forest, where they nest in trees and eat berries. Where people have cut down forests, racoons have adapted to nest in attics, garages and sheds and feed on our leftovers. They have even learned to open gates and rubbish bins with their nimble, grasping hands!

HOW BIODIVERSITY HELPS US

Earth's biodiversity provides us with many of the things that we need to survive. Plants release oxygen when they make their food, giving us the air we breathe, and they provide fuel, fibres and furniture. A third of all species of fruit and vegetable crops would not exist without bees and other pollinators visiting flowers, and around one sixth of the world's people get the protein they need from ocean fish and other seafood. And did you know that many of our medicines, such as aspirin, originally came from plant sources? So, when we bulldoze rainforests and damage other habitats, we also jeopardise our chances of finding cures for other diseases!

BIODIVERSITY SERVICES

The biodiversity that has resulted from evolution also helps us in a variety of ways. Many of the plants that make up water ecosystems help to clean that water. Rotting plants, bacteria, worms and many other organisms help to keep our soil fertile and healthy. Trees and other plants with strong roots bind soil together and prevent erosion during heavy rains or surging seas following storms, protecting us from floods and other natural disasters. Plants absorb gases such as carbon dioxide that contribute to climate change.

Habitats around the world and the plants and animals in them are also very popular holiday destinations. In turn, the tourist industry provides work and money for millions of people.

We take Earth's biodiversity for granted, but nature provides us with all these things for free. If we had to pay for these services, it would cost trillions of pounds!

PROTECTING BIODIVERSITY

It's vitally important to preserve the variety of living things on Earth. Natural selection won't work unless there are a variety of genes giving species the ability to adapt to changing environments. There is no way (yet!) to bring back species that have already become extinct due to human activities, but there are ways we can slow the loss of biodiversity.

WHAT CAN BE DONE?

One way to help is by protecting the places plants and animals live. Governments can create protected areas where people are not allowed to cut down too many trees or take away resources that living things need to survive. They can pass laws to stop people bringing invasive species into their countries. Countries across the world are also looking at ways to slow climate change and reduce pollution, such as using wind power or other alternative sources of energy and building electric cars instead of petrol ones.

WHAT CAN YOU DO?

There is a lot we can do, too. Here are a few ideas. Maybe you can think of some more?

- Reuse, repair or recycle things. This decreases pollution and saves more land being used for waste dumps.
- Use environmentally friendly products.
- Buy local food and foods wrapped in less packaging.
- Buy recycled paper and second-hand wooden furniture to reduce the need to cut down new trees.
- Reduce carbon dioxide emissions by walking, cycling or sharing lifts.

Some countries even go so far as to disinfect landing planes and the shoes of people on them to prevent the arrival of invasive species.

WHAT CAN SCIENCE DO?

Science is finding ways to save endangered species and stop them becoming extinct. Some wild plants and animals are being preserved in zoos, botanical gardens and other safe places. If they also breed successfully in these safe havens and numbers increase, people may release some of them back into the wild. Another method is gene banks. Gene banks are storage facilities that preserve genetic material. Plant seeds can be dried and frozen so they could be studied or even grown again in future. In animals, cells from parent organisms are frozen in special freezers.

Collecting genetic material also makes it easier for scientists to study the DNA of the planet's plants and animals. This could help them work out which genes are responsible for an organism's survival. They could also use genetic engineering to create improved versions of some plants and animals so these species could cope with problems such as climate change. But this is just a possibility. What we know for certain is that we need to save species from extinction now and in the future because biodiversity is vital for evolution and for a healthy planet!

ON KEW!

Kew Gardens in the UK aims to have seeds from a quarter of the world's wild plant species in its Millennium Seed Bank by 2020. That'll be 75,000 species! Fancy labelling that little lot, anyone?

One of the biggest seed banks in the world is deep inside a frozen mountain in the Arctic. It contains more than 800,000 samples and is designed to withstand all natural and human disasters. It's like a modern-day Noah's ark!

EVOLUTION QUIZ!

1. **The book in which Darwin first outlined his theory of evolution was titled:**

   a *Darwin's Diary*

   b *Finding the Finches*

   c *On the Origin of Species*

2. **Which of these is the correct definition of a species?**

   a A group of plants that is safe to eat

   b A way of telling plants from animals

   c A group of animals or plants that share the same characteristics and can reproduce together

3. **Darwin believed that evolution took place:**

   a Quickly

   b Only in the past

   c Gradually, in a series of small changes or steps

4. **What is a fossil?**

   a A model of an extinct animal

   b An actual bone from an extinct animal

   c The remains of a long-dead organism or the imprint left from an organism

5. **What was special about the finches Darwin discovered?**

   a Darwin had never seen finches before

   b They could swim and do tricks

   c Finches on different islands had different beak shapes to eat different foods that were available

6. **Why are there only lemurs on Madagascar?**

   a Lemurs like the sunshine there

   b There were never any lemurs in other parts of the world

   c Lemurs in other parts of the world died out because they faced predators that the lemurs of Madagascar didn't and Madagascan lemurs didn't need to compete with other primates for food

7. **Which one of these is not an example of symbiotic evolution?**

   a Clownfish and anemones

   b Bees and flowers

   c Kittens and koalas

8. **What is natural selection?**

   a The time it takes to choose a new pair of shoes

   b How lions choose which animals will join their pride

   c Nature's way of selecting the best characteristics or features to help a species evolve and survive

9. What were the first living things on planet Earth?

  a Dinosaurs

  b Dragonflies the size of seagulls

  c Single-celled organisms, such as the bacteria that once lived in volcanic pools

10. Why do people think dinosaurs became extinct, about 66 million years ago?

  a They battled each other to death

  b They got too large to find enough food to eat

  c A huge asteroid hit the planet, blocking light and killing plants that fed animals which, in turn, fed the dinosaurs

11. What are antibiotic resistant bacteria?

  a Bacteria that won't do as they are told

  b Bacteria that are used to make medicines

  c Bacteria that evolved so they cannot be killed by antibiotic medicines that used to work on them

12. Which of the following is not an example of artificial selection?

  a Different dog breeds

  b Modern sweetcorn

  c Ants and acacia trees

13. What are clones?

  a People who dress in funny costumes at the circus

  b Robots from the future

  c Individuals that have identical or exactly the same set of genes

14. Why does biodiversity matter?

  a The world would look boring without it

  b There would be no more nature programmes on TV

  c A variety of living things on the Earth is vital for evolution and for our survival

ANSWERS

GLOSSARY

adapt to adjust to new conditions

adaptation a special feature or way of behaving that helps a living thing survive

algae plant-like living thing that can make its own food by photosynthesis. Seaweeds are algae

allergy a reaction that the body has to a particular food or substance

amphibian an animal, such as a frog, that hatches from an egg underwater but lives on land as an adult

ancestor an early type of animal or plant from which others have evolved

antibiotic a medicine used to stop or kill harmful bacteria

arthropod animal of the group that includes insects, spiders, crabs and centipedes

bacteria tiny living things that can help us but that can also cause disease

biodiversity the variety of plant and animal life on Earth

bipedal to walk on two legs

camouflage to blend in or hide against the surroundings

carbon dioxide a gas in the air that contributes to the causes of climate change

carnivore an animal that eats other animals

cell the basic building block of all living things

chromosome the thread-like structure inside a cell that contains its DNA

classify to sort into groups

climate change changes in the world's weather patterns

descendant a person, plant, or animal that is descended from a particular ancestor

DNA a substance that carries genetic information in the cells of plants and animals

ecosystem everything that exists in a particular environment

enzyme a chemical substance that helps animals and plants carry out natural processes, such as digestion

erosion the process by which bits of soil and rock are worn and carried away by water, ice, or wind

evolve to change or develop very gradually over time

extinct no longer in existence, no longer living

fossil the remains of a plant or animal that lived long ago

gene the part of a cell that controls or influences the way a living thing grows or looks etc.

generation a group of plants or animals born and living during the same time

genus a group of related plants or animals that includes several different species

geologist a person who studies rocks and soil

habitat a place or type of place where a group of plants and animals lives

herbicide a chemical used to destroy unwanted plants or weeds

hominid a family of upright bipedal primates that includes modern humans and our extinct ancestors

immune system parts of the body that protect you from diseases and infections

invasive species a type of plant or animal that starts to live in a new place and often causes harm to the original organisms living there

larva a stage of growth of some insects after hatching from an egg

lifecycle the stages in life of a living thing. Living things are born, grow into adults that have their own offspring, and eventually die

mammal an animal that has hair or fur and feeds its young on milk from its body

mineral a solid substance found in nature that is not and never was alive. Rocks are made from minerals.

mollusc group of animals that includes snails, slugs, mussels, and octopuses

multi-cellular made of many cells

nectar a sugary juice found in the centre of a flower

nutrient a substance that organisms need to live

organism a living thing

oxygen a gas in the air around us

parasite a living thing that lives on or in (and usually harms) another living thing

pesticide a chemical used to harm or kill animals that damages plants and crops

pollen a powder or dust at the ends of the male parts of a flower

pollinate to move pollen from the male parts of one flower to the female part of another

pollution when air, soil or water are spoiled or made dirty or harmful by something else

predator an animal that hunts other animals for food

prey an animal that is hunted for food

primate a group of mammals that includes monkeys, apes and humans

reproduce to produce offspring

reptile an animal with hard, scaly skin that lays soft eggs, such as a snake, turtle, or crocodile

sediment tiny pieces of rock, mud, dust or sand

species a group of animals or plants that are similar and can produce young animals or plants

specimen something (such as a fossil or plant) collected as an example of a particular kind of thing

symbiosis the way two different kinds of living things live together and depend on each other

tsunami a giant wave that can cause terrible destruction when it hits land

variation something that is similar to something else but different in some way

vertebrate an animal with a backbone

viral infection a disease caused by a virus (a small living thing that causes diseases)

weathering the wearing away of the surface of rocks by the action of rain, wind, sunlight, or ice

X-ray an image made using invisible light rays that can pass through various objects and that make it possible to see inside things

FIND OUT MORE

Books

The World in Infographics: Our Amazing Planet, Jon Richards and Ed Simkins, Wayland Books, 2014

Mind Webs: Living Things, Anna Claybourne, Wayland Books, 2014

Classification (series), Stephen Savage, Wayland Books, 2014

Infographic Top Ten: Record-Breaking Animals, Jon Richards and Ed Simkins, Wayland Books, 2015

Straight Forward with Science: Classification and Evolution, Peter Riley, Franklin Watts, 2015

Websites

The Natural History Museum website has all sorts of fascinating information and facts about evolution at:

http://www.nhm.ac.uk/nature-online/evolution/

Learn more about your genes and evolution at:

http://www.sciencemuseum.org.uk/on-line/lifecycle/14.asp

Read more about the evolution of humans at:

http://www.bbc.co.uk/sn/prehistoric_life/human/human_evolution/

How good are you at classifying? Try the game at:

http://www.oum.ox.ac.uk/thezone/animals/animalid/games/animal1.htm

Delve deeper into the characteristics of living things at:

http://www.sciencelearn.org.nz/Science-Stories/Earthworms/Characteristics-of-living-things

INDEX

FIND OUT MORE ABOUT EVOLUTION

All you need to know –
from Darwin and genetics to
classification and biodiversity!

the world in infographics
THE NATURAL WORLD
jon richards and ed simkins

978 0 7502 8320 5

Mind Webs
LIVING THINGS
make SCIENCE make SENSE
Anna Claybourne

978 0 7502 8279 6

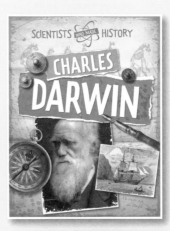

SCIENTISTS WHO MADE HISTORY
CHARLES DARWIN

978 0 7502 8475 2

CLASSIFYING ANIMALS
MAMMALS
Sarah Wilkes

978 0 7502 8485 1

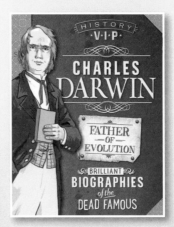

HISTORY V.I.P
CHARLES DARWIN
FATHER OF EVOLUTION
BRILLIANT BIOGRAPHIES of the DEAD FAMOUS

978 0 7502 8849 1